The Quotable Cook

The Quotable Cook

EDITED BY
KATE ROWINSKI

THE LYONS PRESS

FIRST EDITION

Printed in the United States of America

10 9 8 7 6 5 4 3 2 1

Library of Congress Cataloging-in-Publication Data is available on file.

"The majority of those who put together collections of verses or epigrams resemble those who eat cherries or oysters; they begin by choosing the best and end by eating everything."

—Nicolas Chamfort

Table of Contents

An Invitation to Dine

To bring a person into your house is to take charge of his happiness for as long as he is under your roof.

ANTHELME BRILLAT-SAVARIN

Come to dinner! What happier words in the world are there than the invitation to dinner? Nothing bonds people together so much as sitting down to food. We celebrate, mourn together, raise our children, do our business, and debate our deepest convictions—all with food as the centerpiece.

Of course, there are many ways to share a meal. For family, it might be a lazy breakfast on a Sunday morning. Shopping friends make the perfect afternoon luncheon group. Celebrating a new baby may be cause for afternoon tea, while serious celebrations or formal occasions call for an evening dinner. Regardless of your choice, the invitation to dine is a serious commitment.

For the invitee, this commitment carries with it certain responsibilities. They are expected to arrive on time ready to entertain and to be entertained. Pleasantries and small talk are mandatory. The token gift is extended. Gratitude is expressed.

Why take the happiness of someone else into your hands, even for an hour or two? Perhaps it's because, for some of us, the pleasures of sharing a meal are irresistible. The happy contemplation of what food to prepare, the artistry of setting the table, the anticipation of one's friends enjoying each other's company, the soft afterglow of a successful meal. The dinner party is artistry itself, an expression of who you are and what you want to share with others.

In the pages that follow, we'll share the thoughts of a number of experienced diners on the virtues and drawbacks of the invitation to dine, and also the merits of various types of dining occasions.

1

You're Invited

A dinner invitation, once accepted, is a sacred obligation. If you die before the dinner takes place, your executor must attend.

WARD MCALLISTER

Americans are just beginning to regard food the way the French always have. Dinner is not what you do in the evening before something else. Dinner is the evening.

ART BUCHWALD

And do as adversaries do in law; strive mightily, but eat and drink as friends.

WILLIAM SHAKESPEARE
THE TAMING OF THE SHREW

———•••••———

Givers of great dinners know few enemies.

MARTIAL, C. 95 A.D.

———•••••———

If you accept a dinner invitation, you have a moral obligation to be amusing.

THE DUCHESS OF WINDSOR

If you reject the food, ignore the customs, fear the religion and avoid the people, you might better stay home.

JAMES MICHENER

Man loves company even if it is only that of a small burning candle.

GEORG CHRISTOPH LICHTENBERG

No gentleman dines before seven.

OSCAR WILDE

I think this is the most extraordinary collection of talent, of human knowledge, that has ever been gathered together at the White House, with the possible exception of when Thomas Jefferson dined alone.

PRESIDENT JOHN F. KENNEDY
In an address to Nobel Prize winners

The cocktail party ... is a device either for getting rid of social obligations hurriedly en masse or for making overtures toward more serious relationships, as in the etiquette of whoring.

BROOKS ATKINSON

If there is food in the house, a guest is no worry.

PASHTO PROVERB

———•••———

This was a good dinner enough, to be sure: but it was not a dinner to ask a man to.

SAMUEL JOHNSON

———•••———

What dinner parties of the usual kind in country or city would not appear dull to me after all those brilliant ones we gave at the White House?

JULIA GARDINER TYLER

We should look for someone to eat and drink with before looking for something to eat and drink, for dining alone is leading the life of a lion or wolf.

EPICURUS

He who eats alone chokes alone.

PROVERB

Dining is and always was a great artistic opportunity.

FRANK LLOYD WRIGHT

Eating and drinking wants but a beginning.

SCOTTISH PROVERB

You need not rest your reputation on the dinners you give.

HENRY DAVID THOREAU

2

Breakfast, Lunch or Dinner?

All happiness depends on a leisurely breakfast.

JOHN GUNTHER

———•••———

Eat breakfast like a king, lunch like a prince, and dinner like a pauper.

ADELLE DAVIS

———•••———

Hope is a good breakfast, but it is a bad supper.

FRANCIS BACON

It takes some skill to spoil a breakfast—even the English can't do it.

JOHN KENNETH GALBRAITH
ECONOMIST

So in our pride we ordered for breakfast an omelet, toast and coffee and what has just arrived is a tomato salad with onions, a dish of pickles, a big slice of watermelon and two bottles of cream soda.

JOHN STEINBECK
On traveling in the Soviet Union

I am convinced that the Muses and the Graces never thought of having breakfast anywhere but bed.

MARY ARNUM

The walk downstairs to the breakfast table is exercise enough for any gentleman.

CHAUNCEY M. DE PEW

My wife and I tried to breakfast together, but we had to stop or our marriage would have been wrecked.

WINSTON CHURCHILL

Three good meals a day is a bad living.

BENJAMIN FRANKLIN

On a day of fishing there is only one thing over which we have total control, and that is what we have for lunch.

DOUGLAS C. EWING

A good breakfast is no substitute for a large dinner.

CHINESE PROVERB

We plan, we toil, we suffer—in the hope of what? A camel-load of idol's eyes? The title deeds of Radio City? The empire of Asia? A trip to the moon? No, no, no, no. Simply to wake just in time to smell coffee and bacon and eggs.

J. B. PRIESTLY

To eat well in England you should have breakfast three times a day.

SOMERSET MAUGHAM

The crucial period in matrimony is breakfast.

A. P. HERBERT

Manhattan is a narrow island off the coast of New Jersey devoted to the pursuit of lunch.

RAYMOND SOLOKOV

New York is the greatest city in the world for lunch… That's the gregarious time. And when that first martini hits the liver like a silver bullet, there is a sigh of contentment that can be heard in Dubuque.

WILLIAM EMERSON, JR.

You are about to have your first experience with a Greek lunch. I will kill you if you pretend to like it.

JACQUELINE KENNEDY ONASSIS

For a good dinner and a gentle wife you can afford to wait.

DANISH PROVERB

Time is an illusion, lunchtime doubly so.

DOUGLAS ADAMS

———◆◆◆◆———

The good supper is known by its odor.

MOROCCAN PROVERB

———◆◆◆◆———

Once Eve ate the apple, much depends on dinner.

LORD BYRON

———◆◆◆◆———

Everything in France is a pretext for a good dinner.

JEAN ANOUILH

A man seldom thinks with more earnestness of any thing than he does of his dinner.

SAMUEL JOHNSON

———•••———

She had provided a plentiful dinner for them; she wished she could know that they had been allowed to eat it.

JANE AUSTEN
EMMA

———•••———

Anyone who eats three meals a day should understand why cookbooks outsell sex books three to one.

L. M. BOYD

3

Coffee or Tea?

Afternoon tea is probably the simplest fashion in which to exercise hospitality. Pretty cups and saucers are among the possessions of which the young housekeeper has a generous store and they will make an attractive array on her afternoon tea table.

CATHERINE TERHUNE HERRICK

Be kind and courteous to all, even to the stranger from afar. If he says that he is thirsty, give him a cup of tea.

CONFUCIUS

Children are such sticky things, 'specially after tea.

E. F. BROWN

Only Irish coffee provides in a single glass all four essential food groups: alcohol, caffeine, sugar, and fat.

ALEX LEVINE

There is no more wholesome or satisfactory method of entertainment—cheap or dear—than an after-noon tea or noon-day lunch in the woods in fine summer weather.

MARION HARLAND

Drinking a daily cup of tea will surely starve the apothecary.

CHINESE PROVERB

Find yourself a cup of tea; the teapot is behind you. Now tell me about hundreds of things.

SAKI

The pedigree of honey
does not concern the bee;
a clover, any time to him
is aristocracy.

EMILY DICKINSON

Coffee is a beverage that puts one to sleep when not drank.

ALPHONSE ALLAIS

Let me say something about tea. Tea starts bad and never gets better. You put in honey, cream, sugar, lemon and you still go, "Ooh, that's bad."

PAUL REISER

Better to be deprived of food for three days than tea for one.

CHINESE PROVERB

. . . No more shall my teapot so generous be
in filling cups with this pernicious tea,
For I'll fill it with water and drink out the same,
Before I lose Liberty that dearest name.

FROM A LADY'S ADIEU TO HER TEA TABLE,
In support of the boycott of British tea

Coffee falls into the stomach [and] ideas begin to move, things remembered arrive at full gallop [and] the shafts of wit start up like sharp-shooters, similes arrive, the paper is covered with ink.

HONORE DE BALZAC

Nowhere is the English genius of domesticity more notably evident than in the festival of afternoon tea. The mere chink of cups and saucers tunes the mind to happy repose.

GEORGE GISSING

Coffee and tobacco are complete repose.

TURKISH PROVERB

There are few hours in life more agreeable than the hour dedicated to the ceremony known as afternoon tea.

> HENRY JAMES
> *THE PORTRAIT OF A LADY*

———

I hire tea by the tea bag.

> MARTIN AMIS

———

Warm the pot first, please, then put two heaping teaspoonfuls in the pot—no bags—in boiling water, and when it's in, stir it. And when it comes here, I will stir it again.

> LYNN FONTANNE
> On how to make good tea

Stands the church clock at ten to three? And is there honey still for tea?

RUPERT BROOKE

Tea is an affront to lunch and an insult to dinner.

MARK TWAIN

Tea tempers the spirit, harmonizes the mind, dispels lassitude and relieves fatigue, awakens the thought and prevents drowsiness.

LU YU
THE CLASSIC ART OF TEA

Making coffee has become the great compromise of the decade. It's the only thing "real" men do that doesn't seem to threaten their masculinity. To women, it's on the same domestic entry level as putting the spring back into the toilet-tissue holder or taking a chicken out of the freezer to thaw.

ERMA BOMBECK

A woman is like a tea bag—only in hot water do you realize how strong she really is.

NANCY REAGAN

Tea to the English is really a picnic indoors.

ALICE WALKER

———•◦•———

Wash the dishes, wipe the dishes, ring the bell for tea; three good wishes, three good kisses I will give to thee.

NURSERY RHYME

———•◦•———

After a few months' acquaintance with European coffee, one's mind weakens, and he begins to wonder of the rich beverage of home, with its clotted layer of yellow cream on top of it, is not a mere dream after all, and a thing which never existed.

MARK TWAIN

Cocoa? Cocoa! Damn miserable puny stuff; fit for kittens and unwashed boys. Did *Shakespeare* drink cocoa?

SHIRLEY JACKSON

———●·►◄·●———

Coffee? Tea? Me?

JOAN CUSACK
From the movie *Working Girl*

4

The Cook is in the Kitchen

Our lives are not in the laps of the gods, but in the laps of our cooks.

LIN YUTANG

————

Every morning must start from scratch, with nothing on the stoves—that is cuisine.

FERNAND POINT

A good cook is like a sorceress who dispenses happiness.

ELSA SCHIAPARELLI

All are not cooks who carry long knives.

DUTCH PROVERB

In the childhood memories of every good cook, there's a large kitchen, a warm stove, a simmering pot and a mom.

BARBARA COSTIKYAN

Love and eggs are best when they are fresh.

RUSSIAN PROVERB

An unwatched pot boils immediately.

H. F. ELLIS

To get milk and eggs, you must not frighten the cow and hen.

TIBETAN PROVERB

All that is said in the kitchen should not be heard in the parlor.

SCOTTISH PROVERB

An empty belly is the best cook.

ESTONIAN PROVERB

Bringing food alive with your
loving presence.
To have compassion, to have respect
for fresh foods, for broken bowls,
for dirty napkins, and little bugs.

EDWARD ESPE BROWN

Cookery is become an art, a noble science; cooks are gentlemen.

ROBERT BURTON

Cookery means the knowledge of Medea and of Circe and of Helen and of the Queen of Sheba.

JOHN RUSKIN

Cooking is like love. It should be entered into with abandon or not at all.

HARRIET VAN HORNE

The qualities of an exceptional cook are akin to those of a successful tightrope walker; an abiding passion for the task, courage to go out on a limb and an impeccable sense of balance.

BRYAN MILLER

Do that in less time than it takes to cook asparagus.

ROMAN PROVERB

Do you want to make a tamale with peanut butter and jelly? Go ahead! Somebody will eat it.

BOBBY FLAY

Fish, to taste right, must swim three times—in water, in butter, and in wine.

POLISH PROVERB

Anybody can make you enjoy the first bite of a dish, but only a real chef can make you enjoy the last.

FRANCOIS MINOT

Food prepared by two cooks is neither hot nor cold.

TALMUD

Governing a great nation is like cooking a small dish—too much handling will spoil it.

LAO-TZU

I am not a good cook.

MAMIE EISENHOWER

I could cook a little but, I must confess, I was never a great success at it.

GRACE COOLIDGE

I like a cook who smiles out loud when he tastes his own work. Let God worry about your modesty, I want to see your enthusiasm.

ROBERT FARRAR CAPON

If the spit is right, then the meat is right.

INDIAN PROVERB

If you want to make an apple pie from scratch, you must first create the universe.

CARL SAGAN

In the end, your creativity—perhaps even your outrageousness—will determine the final result.

BOBBY FLAY

Let wine add its savor to soups, fish sauces, meat, game and desserts; there is a subtlety about it that is indescribable.

DIONE LUCAS
THE CORDON BLEU COOKBOOK

I don't even butter my bread; I consider that cooking.

KATHERINE CEBRIAN

I see him even now going the way of all flesh, that is to say towards the kitchen.

JOHN WEBSTER

My cooking was and still is about the worst in America. George is so kind about it.

BARBARA BUSH

No mean woman can cook well, for it calls for a light head, a generous spirit and a large heart.

PAUL GAUGIN

Non cooks think it is silly to invest two hours work in two minutes enjoyment, but if cooking is evanescent, so is the ballet.

JULIA CHILD

Often, admiring a chef and getting to know him is like loving goose liver and then meeting the goose.

GEORGE LANG

Several years ago *Life* had a picture story on how to skin an eel. I trust everyone cut it out and put it in his files.

JAMES BEARD

Cooking is not simply in the tongue,
in the palate.
It is in the whole body
flowing out of the groin and chest
through arms and hands.

EDWARD ESPE BROWN

There is no technique, there is just the way to do it.
Now, are we going to measure or are we going to
cook?

FRANCES MAYES
UNDER THE TUSCAN SUN

If people take the trouble to cook, you should take
the trouble to eat.

ROBERT MORLEY

Simple cooking cannot be trusted to a simple cook.

COUNTESS MORPHE

Summer cooking implies a sense of immediacy, a capacity to capture the essence of the fleeting moment.

ELIZABETH DAVID

The torch of love is lit in the kitchen.

FRENCH PROVERB

This is every cook's opinion—
no savory dish without an onion,
but lest your kissing should be spoiled
your onions must be fully boiled.

JONATHAN SWIFT

'Tis an ill cook that cannot lick his own fingers.

WILLIAM SHAKESPEARE

Too many cooks spoil the broth.

ENGLISH PROVERB

Murder is commoner among cooks than among members of any other profession.

W. H. AUDEN

We need more cooks, not more cookbooks.

CHARLES V. W. BROOKS

What I go for in my cooking is sinful, bold and real.

EMERIL LAGASSE

The biggest seller is cookbooks and the second is diet books—how not to eat what you've just learned how to cook.

ANDY ROONEY

What is literature compared with cooking? The one is shadow, the other is substance.

E.V. LUCAS

What my mother believed about cooking is that if you worked hard and prospered, someone else would do it for you.

NORA EPHRON

I never go into the kitchen.

> LOU HENRY HOOVER
> When the new First Lady Eleanor Roosevelt
> asked her to show her the White House kitchen.

What I am jazzed about is knowing that this is a new week, and Mother Nature's making new ingredients.

> EMERIL LAGASSE

An Englishman teaching an American about food is like the blind leading the one-eyed.

> A. J. LIEBLING

I refuse to believe that trading recipes is silly. Tuna fish casserole is at least as real as corporate stock.

BARBARA GRIZZUTI HARRISON

It's more useful to have knowledge about cuts of meat than a lot of money.

JACQUES PEPIN

I was 32 when I started cooking; until then I just ate.

JULIA CHILD

We're not building a rocket ship here, we're cooking—plain and simple.

EMERIL LAGASSE

I was determined to know beans.

HENRY DAVID THOREAU

If you are lazy and dump everything together, they won't come out as well as if you add one thing at a time. It's like everything else; no shortcuts without compromising quality.

LIONEL POILANE

If you must cook,
please offer yourself
a substantial piece of emptiness.
Hold back nothing,
until you experience offering,
"Eat me! And be nourished."

EDWARD ESPE BROWN
THE TASSAJARA BREAD BOOK

When love and skill work together, expect a master-piece.

JOHN RUSKIN

There is one thing more exasperating than a wife who can cook and won't, and that's a wife who can't cook and will.

ROBERT FROST

The time of business does not with me differ from the time of prayer, and in the noise and clatter of my kitchen . . . I possess God in as great tranquility as if I were upon my knees at the Blessed Sacrament.

BROTHER LAWRENCE (17TH CENTURY)

The only good thing about him is his cook. The world visits his dinners, not him.

MOLIERE

The only real stumbling block is the fear of failure. In cooking, you've got to have a what-the-hell attitude.

JULIA CHILD

That Tuscan cooking has remained so simple is a long tribute to the abilities of peasant women who cooked so well, that no one, even now, wants to veer into new directions.

FRANCES MAYES

The definitive recipe for any Italian dish has not yet appeared. We are still creating.

LUIGI BARZINI

The discovery of a new dish does more for human happiness than the discovery of a new star.

ANTHELME BRILLAT-SAVARIN

There is no sight on earth more appealing than the sight of a woman making dinner for someone she loves.

THOMAS WOLFE

The man with meat seeks fire.

NIGERIAN PROVERB

If you can organize your kitchen, you can organize your life.

LOUIS PARRISH

The most remarkable thing about my mother is that for thirty years she served the family nothing but leftovers. The original meal has never been found.

CALVIN TRILLIN

The taste of the kitchen is better than the smell.

THOMAS FULLER

If you want to be real technical on the subject, while all soul food is southern food, not all southern food is 'soul'.

BOB JEFFRIES

In Mexico we have a word for sushi: bait.

JOSÉ SIMONS

Kissing don't last: cookery do!

GEORGE MEREDITH

There has always been a food processor in the kitchen. But once upon a time she was usually called the missus, or Mom.

SUE BERKMAN

Rice is born in water and must die in wine.

ITALIAN PROVERB

There is no such thing as a pretty good omelette.

FRENCH PROVERB

5

The Gourmet

Actually, the true gourmet, like the true artist, is one of the unhappiest creatures existent. His trouble comes from so seldom finding what he constantly seeks—perfection.

LUDWIG BEMELMANS

Gourmet: Usually little more than a glutton festooned with credit cards.

SYDNEY J. HARRIS

The golden rule when reading the menu is, if you cannot pronounce it, you cannot afford it.

FRANK MUIR

Cuisine is when things taste like themselves.

CURNONSKY

A daydream is a meal at which images are eaten. Some of us are gourmets, some gourmands, and a good many take their images precooked out of a can and swallow them down whole, absent-mindedly and with little relish.

W. H. AUDEN

Great food is like great sex. The more you have the more you want.

GAEL GREENE

A gourmet who thinks of calories is like a tart, who looks at her watch.

JAMES BEARD

A gourmet is just a glutton with brains.

PHILLIP HABERMAN, JR.

For nothing keeps a poet
in his high singing mood
like unappeasable hunger
for unattainable food.

JOYCE KILMER

How can they say my life is not a success? Have I not for more than sixty years got enough to eat and escaped being eaten?

LOGAN SMITH

Whenever I get married, I start buying *Gourmet* magazine.

NORA EPHRON

Give me books, French wine and fine weather, and a little music out of doors, played by someone I do not know.

JOHN KEATS

Beneath these green mountains where spring rules the year,
the irbarbutus and loquat in season appear,
And feasting on lychee—300 a day,
I shouldn't mind staying eternally here.

SU SHIH

Eating is not merely a material pleasure. Eating well gives a spectacular joy to life and contributes immensely to goodwill and happy companionship. It is of great importance to the morale.

ELSA SCHIAPARELLI

EPICURE: One who gets nothing better than the cream of everything, but cheerfully makes the best of it.

OLIVER HEREFORD

As life's pleasures go, food is second only to sex. Except for salami and eggs. Now that's better than sex, but only if the salami is thickly sliced.

ALAN KING

Your eyes are always bigger than your stomach.

CONFUCIUS

I am not a glutton—I am an explorer of food.

ERMA BOMBECK

He who distinguishes the true savor of his food can never be a glutton; he who does not cannot be otherwise.

HENRY DAVID THOREAU

I'm at the age where food has taken the place of sex in my life. In fact, I've just had a mirror put over my kitchen table.

RODNEY DANGERFIELD

I don't like gourmet cooking, or "this" cooking or "that" cooking. I like "good" cooking.

JAMES BEARD

Food is an important part of a balanced diet.

FRAN LEBOWITZ

Why does man kill? He kills for food. And not only food: frequently there must be a beverage.

WOODY ALLEN

I said to my friends that if I was going to starve, I might as well starve where the food is good.

VIRGIL THOMSON
On life in Paris as a young man

The French cook: [the English] open tins.

JOHN GALSWORTHY

I, Madam, who live at a variety of good tables, am a much better judge of cookery, than any person who has a very tolerable cook, but lives much at home.

SAMUEL JOHNSON

It is good food and not fine words that keep me alive.

MOLIERE

Never eat anything you can't lift.

MISS PIGGY

I've been on a diet for two weeks and all I've lost is two weeks.

TOTIE FIELDS

In department stores, so much kitchen equipment is bought indiscriminately by people who just come in for men's underwear.

JULIA CHILD

Looks can be deceiving, it's eating that's believing.

JAMES THURBER

After eating, an *epicure* gives a thin smile of satisfaction; a *gastronome*, burping into his napkin, praises the food in a magazine; a *gourmet*, repressing his burp, criticizes the food in the same magazine; a *gourmand* belches happily and tells everybody where he ate; a *glutton* embraces the white porcelain alter, or more plainly, he barfs.

WILLIAM SAFIRE

There is no love sincerer than the love of food.

GEORGE BERNARD SHAW

The most indispensable quality in a cook is punctuality, and no less is required of a guest.

ANTHELME BRILLAT-SAVARIN

The Guest List

HOSPITALITY, n. The virtue which induces us to feed and lodge certain persons who are not in need of food and lodging.

AMBROSE BIERCE
THE DEVIL'S DICTIONARY, 1911

There is some sort of force at work that causes us to want to connect with each other through food. We take great pleasure in asking people to dine with us, and go to great lengths to ensure a perfect meal, and a perfect evening.

The diners make up a diverse group, for whom the simple act of eating is very personal. They like their meals designed to their tastes, and everyone arrives anticipating something different. Not all guests, though, are happy to simply be invited, there is, inevitably, a gourmet present—the one whose business it is to determine whether our food is worth enjoying. He is not critical simply for the sake of being contrary, he is, instead, the counterpoint to the chef, the other person present who really thinks about the food, who savors the chef's artistry and understands his motives.

And then there is the host or hostess, the person whose job it is to spread hospitality through the room, find common topics of conversation for strangers, smooth ruffled feathers between family members, and, generally, make sure that everyone is happy.

In the pages that follow, join us for dinner, and share the thoughts of a diverse group of thinkers—from differing cultures, eras, and backgrounds—on the universal subject of cooking, food, and entertaining.

6

Hospitality

At a dinner party one should eat wisely but not too well, and talk well but not too wisely.

Somerset Maugham

—————

Conversation is the enemy of good wine and food.

Alfred Hitchcock

—————

Wit is the salt of conversation, not the food.

William Hazlitt

A smiling face is half the meal.

LATVIAN PROVERB

After a good dinner, one can forgive anybody, even one's relations.

OSCAR WILDE

On the continent people have good food; in England people have good table manners.

GEORGE MIKES

Elegance is the art of not astonishing.

JEAN COCTEAU

Grilling means good times, good friends, and hopefully, great food.

BOBBY FLAY

Is it not delightful to have friends coming from distant quarters?

Confucius

His house was perfect, whether you like food, or sleep, or work, or story-telling, or singing, or just sitting and thinking best, or a pleasant mixture of them all.

J. R. R. TOLKEIN
THE HOBBIT

Eating and scratching want but a beginning.

ROMANIAN PROVERB

But when the time comes that a man has had his dinner, then the true man comes to the surface.

MARK TWAIN

When planning a dinner party, what's more important than what's on the table is what's on the chairs.

W. S. GILBERT

Don't let love interfere with your appetite. It never does with mine.

ANTHONY TROLLOPE

Food had something of a sacred function in Greensboro. It was not just something that assuaged our hunger while we concentrated on something else, but was a reality that that lived in every moment it was prepared and eaten.

LUANN LANDON
DINNER AT MISS LADY'S

I asked him, if he ever huffed his wife about his dinner? "So often (replied he), that at last she called to me, and said, Nay, hold Mr. Johnson, do not make a farce of thanking God for a dinner which in a few moments you will protest not eatable."

PIOZZI

I went to dinner, which was served in a small private room of the club with the usual piano and fiddlers present to make conversation difficult and comfort impossible.

MARK TWAIN

If you haven't got anything nice to say about any-body, come sit next to me.

ALICE ROOSEVELT LONGWORTH

It is not the quantity of the meat, but the cheerful-ness of the guests, which makes the feast.

EDWARD HYDE

I'd rather have roses on my table than diamonds on my neck.

EMMA GOLDMAN

Above all, do not fail to give good dinners, and to pay attention after the ladies.

NAPOLEON BONAPARTE

Like a good pioneer, Father hankered to eat outdoors. And he ate outdoors, come gale, come zephyr.

ROBERT P. TRISTAN COFFIN

No man is lonely while eating spaghetti—it requires too much attention.

CHRISTOPHER MORLEY

Our eyes must have their share.

ITALIAN PROVERB

Small cheer and great welcome makes a merry feast.

WILLIAM SHAKESPEARE

That old English saying: After dinner sit a while, and after supper walk a mile.

THOMAS COGAN

To offer wine is the most charming gesture of hospitality, and a host brings out for his guests the finest he has.

ALEXIS LICHINE

When eating bamboo sprouts, remember the man who planted them.

CHINESE PROVERB

When my mother had to get dinner for 8 she'd make enough for 16 and only serve half.

GRACIE ALLEN

Laughter is brightest where food is best.

IRISH PROVERB

Music with dinner is an insult both to the cook and the violinist.

G. K. CHESTERTON

The cocktail party is probably America's greatest contribution to the world of entertaining.

MARTHA STEWART

The hostess must be like the duck—calm and un-ruffled on the surface, and paddling like hell under-neath.

ANONYMOUS

The hour of dinner includes everything of sensual and intellectual gratification which a great nation glories in producing.

SYDNEY SMITH

The way to a man's heart is through his stomach.

FANNY FERN

———◆◆◆———

There is an emanation for the heart in genuine hospitality which cannot be described but is immediately felt, and puts the stranger at once at his ease.

WASHINGTON IRVING

7

A Loaf of Bread . . .

A crust eaten in peace is better than a banquet par-
taken in anxiety.

AESOP

———•••———

All sorrows are less with bread.

MIGUEL DE CERVANTES
DON QUIXOTE

Go thy way, eat thy bread with joy, and drink thy wine with a merry heart; for God now accepteth thy works.

ECCLESIASTES 9:7

A piece of bread in one's pocket is better than a feather in one's cap.

SWEDISH PROVERB

And the best bread was of my mother's own making—the best in all the land.

SIR HENRY JAMES
OLD MEMORIES

A bagel is a doughnut with the sin removed.

GEORGE ROSENBAUM

Eat bread with pleasure, drink wine by measure.

FRENCH PROVERB

Man does live by bread alone, even presliced bread.

D. W. BROGAN

Better bread with water than cake with trouble.

RUSSIAN PROVERB

Bread deals with living things, with giving life, with growth, with the seed, the grain that nurtures. It is not coincidence that we say bread is the staff of life.

LIONEL POILANE

It requires a certain kind of mind to see beauty in a hamburger bun.

RAY KROC
Founder, McDonald's

Cast thy bread upon the waters, for thou shalt find it after many days.

ECCLESIASTES

Good bread is the most fundamentally satisfying of all foods; and good bread with fresh butter, the greatest of feasts.

JAMES BEARD

———

Bread is the warmest, kindest of words. Write it always with a capital letter, like your own name.

ANONYMOUS

———

Here is bread which strengthens man's heart, and therefore called the staff of life.

MATTHEW HENRY

Everything revolves around bread and death.

JEWISH PROVERB

I know on which side my bread is buttered.

JOHN HEYWOOD

I do like a little bit of butter to my bread.

A. A. MILNE
WHEN WE WERE VERY YOUNG

A philosopher is a person who doesn't care which side his bread is buttered on; he knows he eats both sides anyway.

JOYCE BROTHERS

The rule is jam tomorrow and jam yesterday, but never jam today.

LEWIS CARROLL
ALICE IN WONDERLAND

What is life without jam?

JAMES ELROY FLECKER

Marmalade in the morning has the same effect on taste buds that a cold shower has on the body.

JEANINE LARMOTH

I like reality that tastes like bread.

JEAN ANOUILH

My piece of bread only belongs to me when I know that everyone else has a share, and that no one starves while I eat.

LEO TOLSTOY

With bread and wine you can walk your road.

SPANISH PROVERB

Bread is the king of the table and all else is merely the court that surrounds the king. The countries are the soup, the meat, the vegetables, the salad ... but bread is king.

LOUIS BROMFIELD

Without bread and wine, even love will pine.

FRENCH PROVERB

I have trouble with toast. Toast is very difficult. You have to watch it all the time or it burns up.

JULIA CHILD

You can travel fifty thousand miles in America without once tasting a piece of good bread.

HENRY MILLER

Malta is the only country in the world where the local delicacy is the bread.

ALAN COREN

Whose bread I eat, his song I sing.

GERMAN PROVERB

When you have bread, do not look for cake.

POLISH PROVERB

We want bread and roses too.

SLOGAN OF WOMEN STRIKERS
LAWRENCE, MASSACHUSETTS

The smell of bread baking, like the sound of lightly flowing water, is indescribable in its evocation of innocence and delight.

M. F. K. FISHER

Make bread while the oven is hot.

ITALIAN PROVERB

There's nothing like unrequited love to take all the pleasure out of a peanut butter sandwich.

CHARLES M. SCHULTZ

They that have much butter, may lay it thick on their bread.

SCOTTISH PROVERB

They touched earth and grain grew.

MARGARET ABIGAIL WALKER

Too few people understand a really good sandwich.

JAMES BEARD

When you have only two pennies left in the world, buy a loaf of bread with one, and a lily with the other.

CHINESE PROVERB

8

. . . and a Jug of Wine

Champagne has the taste of an apple peeled with a steel knife.

ALDOUS HUXLEY

———◆✦◆———

Claret is the liquor for boys; port for men; but he who aspires to be a hero must drink brandy.

SAMUEL JOHNSON

Short-term amnesia is not the worst affliction if you have an Irish flair for the sauce.

NORMAN MAILER

———

Alcohol removes inhibitions—like that scared little mouse who got drunk and shook his whiskers and shouted: 'Now bring on that damn cat!'

ELEANOR EARLY

———

A meal without wine is like a day without sunshine.

ANTHELME BRILLAT-SAVARIN

I never drink anything stronger than gin before breakfast.

W. C. FIELDS

Well, between Scotch and nothin', I suppose I'd take Scotch. It's the nearest thing to good moonshine I can find.

WILLIAM FAULKNER

No nation is drunken where wine is cheap . . . it is, in truth, the only antidote to the bane of whiskey.

THOMAS JEFFERSON

Drunkenness is nothing but voluntary madness.

SENECA

Chardonnay is a red wine masquerading as a white, and Pinot Noir is a white wine masquerading as a red.

ANDRE TCHELISTCHEFF

———•••••———

One third of a tumbler filled with raspberry vinegar—add ice, a teaspoon of sugar and top with carbonated water. Garnish with fresh berries and a mint leaf.

MARY RANDOLPH
THE VIRGINIA HOUSEWIFE

———•••••———

What two ideas are more inseparable than beer and Britannia?

REVEREND SYDNEY SMITH

Eating teaches drinking.

ITALIAN PROVERB

———◆•••◆———

Work is the curse of the drinking class.

OSCAR WILDE

———◆•••◆———

The condition of inebriation is very nearly a universal experience and the words come from all our societal venues—the fraternity house, debutante ball, literary luncheon, longshoreman's bar, the Wild West.

BRUCE WEBER

This is one of the disadvantages of wine: it makes a man mistake words for thought.

SAMUEL JOHNSON

Champagne, if you are seeking the truth, is better than a lie detector. It encourages a man to be expansive, even reckless, while lie detectors are only a challenge to tell lies successfully.

GRAHAM GREENE

They who drink beer will think beer.

WASHINGTON IRVING

I envy people who drink—at least they know what to blame everything on.

OSCAR LEVANT

You must be careful about giving any drink whatsoever to a bore. A lit-up bore is the worst in the world.

DAVID CECIL

Religions change, but beer and wine remain.

ANONYMOUS

I have taken more good from alcohol than alcohol has taken from me.

WINSTON CHURCHILL

Wine is bottled poetry.

ROBERT LOUIS STEVENSON

Burgundy makes you think of silly things; Bordeaux makes you talk about them, and Champagne makes you do them.

ANTHELME BRILLAT-SAVARIN

It is better to hide ignorance, but it is hard to do this when we relax over wine.

HERACLITUS

Wine gives courage and makes men more apt for passion.

OVID

Vodka is the aunt of wine.

RUSSIAN PROVERB

Friendships develop over food and wine.

PRINCE NICHOLAS ROMANOFF

The best wine is the oldest, the best water the
newest.

WILLIAM BLAKE

Wine is sure proof that God loves us and wants us
to be happy.

BENJAMIN FRANKLIN

Wine is sunlight, held together by water.

GALILEO

The night they invented champagne, it's plain as it can be. They thought of you and me.

ALLAN JAY LERNER AND FREDERICK LOEW

———

For when the wine is in, the wit is out.

THOMAS BECON

———

A thousand cups of wine do not suffice when friends meet, but half a sentence is too much when there is no meeting of minds.

CHINESE PROVERB

Music is the wine that fills the cup of silence.

ROBERT FRIPP

What is the definition of good wine? It should start and end with a smile.

WILLIAM SOKOLIN

Wine is the best of all medicines and the worst of all poisons.

JAPANESE PROVERB

If I didn't have a problem with alcohol, I'd drink all the time.

HAVELOCK ELLIS

The Menu

The culmination of the day's events is here. Dinner is served. Everyone involved is abuzz with anticipation. Diners come to the table and praise the crystal and the flowers; they evaluate the seating arrangements, and settle themselves comfortably for the moment at hand. Aromas waft from the kitchen as the final banging of pots and clinking of dishes announces the arrival of the meal.

A graceful dinner begins slowly, like a well-written symphony. Appetizers appear—nibbles of savory bites to whet our appetites, stimulate conversation and build anticipation. Soup appears next—steaming platters that simultaneously comfort and cheer the guests, light salad may arrive—and then a cool punctuation mark that cleanses the palette and prepares you for what's to come.

The evening party builds with every course. Wine is poured and bread is passed. The main course is at hand. What will it be? Truffled beef and grilled vegetables? Roasted quail and saffron rice?

Plates are cleared and glasses refilled. The cheeses and fruits come out, and guests nibble again, allowing their palates to be drawn back for just one more taste. Dessert caps off the evening, with coffee, tea or brandy. Hours have passed, another pleasant evening spent with friends and family.

9

Appetizers

The greatest dishes are very simple dishes.

ESCOFFIER

Appetizers are the little things you keep eating until you lose your appetite.

JOE MOORE

It's so beautifully arranged on the plate—you know somebody's fingers have been all over it.

JULIA CHILD

A pate is nothing more than a French meatloaf that's had a couple of cocktails.

CAROL CUTLER

How do they taste? They taste like more.

H. L. MENCKEN

He was a very valiant man who first adventured on eating oysters.

JAMES I

———•·•·•———

I will not eat oysters. I want my food dead—not sick, not wounded—dead.

WOODY ALLEN

———•·•·•———

If you don't love life you can't enjoy an oyster; there is a shock of freshness to it and intimations of the ages of man, some piercing intuition of the sea and all its weeds and breezes. [They] shiver you for a split second.

ELEANOR CLARK

Life is like a box of sardines and we are all looking for the key.

ALAN BENNETT

If I had a son who was ready to marry, I would tell him, 'Beware of girls who don't like wine, truffles, cheese, or music.'

COLETTE

Life is too short to stuff a mushroom.

SHIRLEY CONRAN

Oysters are the usual opening to a winter break-fast . . . indeed, they are almost indispensable.

ALMANACH DES GOURMANDES

I think somebody should come up with a way to breed a very large shrimp. That way, you could ride him, then, after you camped at night, you could eat him. How about it, science?

JACK HANDEY

If I can't have too many truffles, I'll do without.

COLETTE

Our minds are like our stomachs; they are whetted by the change of their food, and variety supplies both with fresh appetites.

MARCUS FABIUS QUINTILLIAN

No man in the world has more courage than the man who can stop after eating one peanut.

CHANNING POLLOCK

Almost every person has something secret he likes to eat.

M. F. K. FISHER

I don't like to eat snails. I prefer fast food.

STRANGE DE JIM

Thou shalt not serve pasta on the same plate or at the same time, even on a side plate, with other foods.

LORENZA DE'MEDICI

Bachelor's fare: bread and cheese, and kisses.

JONATHAN SWIFT

Why, then the world's mine oyster, which I with sword will open.

WILLIAM SHAKESPEARE
THE MERRY WIVES OF WINDSOR

10

Soup or Salad

It takes four men to dress a salad: a wise man for the salt, a madman for the pepper, a miser for the vinegar, and a spendthrift for the oil.

<small>ANONYMOUS</small>

———◦••◦———

The better the salad, the worse the dinner.

<small>ITALIAN PROVERB</small>

He who gives up olive oil gives up his good taste.

FRENCH PROVERB

A cucumber should be well sliced, and dressed with pepper and vinegar, and then thrown out.

SAMUEL JOHNSON

The West wasn't won on salad.

NORTH DAKOTA BEEF COUNCIL

You don't win friends with salad.

HOMER SIMPSON

To make a good salad is to be a brilliant diplomat—
to know how much oil to put with one's vinegar.

OSCAR WILDE

———

The embarrassing thing is that the salad dressing is
out-grossing my films.

PAUL NEWMAN

———

Eat watercress and gain wit.

GREEK PROVERB

———

Hey, salads don't have to be boring, they can be
wild!

EMERIL LAGASSE

Beautiful soup! Who cares for fish, game or any other dish? Who would not give all else for two pennyworth only of beautiful soup?

LEWIS CARROLL
ALICE IN WONDERLAND

Borscht and bread make your cheeks red.

JEWISH FOLK SAYING

Chowder breathes reassurance. It steams consolation.

CLEMENTINE PADDLEFORD

Eat bad soup with a big spoon.

ARMENIAN PROVERB

My good health is due to a soup made of white doves. It is simply wonderful as a tonic.

CHIANG KAI-SHEK

Good soup draws the chair to it.

GHANIAN PROVERB

I believe I once considerably scandalized her by declaring that clear soup was a more important factor in life than a clear conscience.

SAKI

I live on good soup, not on fine words.

MOLIERE

Onion stew sustains. The process of making it is somewhat like the process of learning to love. It requires commitment, extraordinary effort, time, and will make you cry.

RONNI LUNDY

I would like to find a stew that gives me heartburn immediately, instead of at three o'clock in the morning.

JOHN BARRYMORE

Talk of joy: there may be things better than beef stew and baked potatoes and home made bread—there may be.

DAVID GRAYSON

We are always giving foreign names to very native things. I believe that what we call Irish stew might more properly called English stew, and that it is not particularly familiar in Ireland.

G. K. CHESTERTON

If you miss the meat, take the soup.

LEBANESE PROVERB

It breathes reassurance, it offers consolation; after a weary day it promotes sociability. . . . There is nothing like a bowl of hot soup...

LOUIS DEGOUY
THE SOUP BOOK

Of all the items on the menu, soup is that which exacts the most delicate perfection and the strictest attention.

AUGUSTE ESCOFFIER

A first-rate soup is more creative than a second-rate painting.

ABRAHAM MASLOW

No, I don't take soup. You can't build a meal on a lake.

ELSIE DE WOLFE (LADY MENDL)

Of soup and love, the first is best.

THOMAS FULLER

Only the pure in heart can make a good soup.

LUDWIG VAN BEETHOVEN

———•••••———

Soup and fish explain half the emotions of human life.

SYDNEY SMITH

———•••••———

The best kind of onion soup is the simplest kind.

AMBROSE BIERCE

———•••••———

The first sip of broth is always the hottest.

IRISH PROVERB

The more the eggs, the thicker the soup.

SERBIAN PROVERB

To make a good soup, the pot must only simmer or "smile".

FRENCH PROVERB

Worries go down better with soup.

JEWISH PROVERB

11

Tonight's Vegetable

Beets, emollient, nutritive, and relaxing.

JOHN ARBUTHNOT

———•·•·•———

Cauliflower is nothing but cabbage with a college education.

MARK TWAIN

Eat no onions nor garlic, for we are to utter sweet breath.

WILLIAM SHAKESPEARE

Happy is said to be the family which can eat onions together. They are, for the time being, separate, from the world, and have a harmony of aspiration.

CHARLES DUDLEY WARNER

How luscious lies the pea within the pod.

EMILY DICKINSON

Asparagus, when picked, should be no thicker than a darning needle.

ALICE B. TOKLAS

Life is like eating artichokes; you have got to go through so much to get so little.

THOMAS ALOYSIUS DORGAN

I am not a vegetarian because I love animals. I am a vegetarian because I hate plants.

A. WHITNEY BROWN

Nothing will benefit human health and increase the chances for survival of life on Earth as much as the evolution to a vegetarian diet.

ALBERT EINSTEIN

I was a vegetarian until I started leaning toward the sunlight.

RITA RUDNER

I stick to asparagus which still seems to inspire gentle thought.

CHARLES LAMB

I do not like broccoli and I haven't liked it since I was a little kid and my mother made me eat it. And I'm President of the United States and I'm not going to eat any more broccoli.

PRESIDENT GEORGE BUSH

It's no use boiling your cabbage twice.

IRISH PROVERB

Let onion atoms lurk within the bowl
And, half suspected animate the whole.

SYDNEY SMITH

Let the sky rain potatoes.

WILLIAM SHAKESPEARE
THE MERRY WIVES OF WINDSOR

Public and private food in America has become eat-able, here and there extremely good. Only the fried potatoes go unchanged, as deadly as before.

LUIGI BARZINI

The first zucchini I ever saw I killed it with a hoe.

JOHN GOULD
MONSTROUS DEPRAVITY, 1963

Spinach: Divide into little piles. Rearrange again into new piles. After five or six maneuvers, sit back and say you are full.

DELIA EPHRON

Plant a radish, get a radish, never any doubt. That's why I love vegetables, you know what they're about!

TOM JONES AND HARVEY SCHMIDT

The bittersweet of a white oak acorn which you nibble in a bleak November walk over the tawny earth is more to me than a slice of imported pineapple.

HENRY DAVID THOREAU

These perforated brown-white asparagus tips—these morels, smelling of wet graham crackers mixed with maple leaves.

WILLIAM JAY SMITH

The sliced onions give of their essence after a brew and becomes the ambrosia for gods and men.

JANE BOTHWELL

Only strangers eat tamarinds—but they only eat them once.

MARK TWAIN

What was paradise, but a garden full of vegetables and herbs and pleasure? Nothing there but delights.

WILLIAM LAWSON

Up from the meadows
rich with corn.
Clear is the cool
September morn.

JOHN GREENLEAF WHITTIER

We don't care to eat toadstools that think they are truffles.

MARK TWAIN

What I say is that, if a man really likes potatoes, he must be a pretty decent sort of fellow.

A. A. MILNE

It is a mistake to think you can solve any major problems just with potatoes.

DOUGLAS ADAMS

Found a little patched-up inn in the village of Bul-son . . . Proprietor had nothing but potatoes; but what a feast he laid before me. Served them in five different courses . . . It may be because I had not eaten for 36 hours, but that meal seems about the best I ever had.

DOUGLAS MACARTHUR

Spinach is the broom of the stomach.

FRENCH PROVERB

Nature alone is antique and the oldest art is mushroom.

THOMAS CARLYLE

12

Dinner is Served

A dish fit for the gods.

WILLIAM SHAKESPEARE

———•••———

If they like it, it serves four; otherwise, six.

ELSIE ZUSSMAN

———•••———

Tis not the meat, but 'tis the appetite makes eating a delight.

SIR JOHN SUCKLING

My doctor told me to stop having intimate dinners for four. Unless there are three other people.

ORSON WELLES

———•••——

When we lose, I eat. When we win, I eat. I also eat when we're rained out.

TOMMY LASORDA
Former manager of the Los Angeles Dodgers

———•••——

I want a dish to taste good, rather than to have been seethed in pig's milk and served wrapped in a rhubarb leaf with grated thistle root.

KINGSLEY AMIS

I never see any home cooking. All I get is fancy stuff.

PRINCE PHILIP
DUKE OF EDINBURGH

At the inn where we stopped he was exceedingly dissatisfied with some roast mutton we had for dinner. . . . He scolded the waiter, saying, "It is as bad as bad can be: it is ill-fed, ill-killed, ill-kept, and ill-drest."

SAMUEL JOHNSON

If I have done the hardest possible day's work, and then come to sit down in a corner and eat my supper comfortably—why, then I don't think I deserve any reward for my hard day's work—for am I not now at peace? Is not my supper good?

HERMAN MELVILLE

Carve a ham as if you were shaving the face of a friend.

HENRI CHARPENTIER

———•••••———

Everything you see I owe to spaghetti.

SOPHIA LOREN

———•••••———

I come from a home where gravy is a beverage.

ERMA BOMBECK

———•••••———

If Beef's the King of Meat, Potato's Queen of the World.

IRISH PROVERB

Nothing would be more tiresome than eating and drinking if God had not made them a pleasure as well as a necessity.

VOLTAIRE

Most turkeys taste better the day after; my mother's tasted better the day before.

RITA RUDNER

My mother's menu consisted of two choices: Take it or leave it.

BUDDY HACKETT

Poultry is for the cook what canvas is for the painter.

ANTHELME BRILLAT-SAVARIN

When a poor man eats a chicken, one of them is sick.

YIDDISH PROVERB

One sits the whole day at the desk and appetite is standing next to me. 'Away with you,' I say. But Comrade Appetite does not budge from the spot.

LEONID BREZHNEV
FORMER SOVIET PREMIER

Rice and fish are as inseparable as mother and child.

VIETNAMESE PROVERB

If it weren't for Philo T. Farnsworth, inventor of the television, we'd still be eating frozen radio dinners.

JOHNNY CARSON

Winter food here recalls the hunter stepping in the door with his jacket pockets filled with birds, the farmer bringing in the olive harvest and beginning the cold-weather work of cleaning the trees, trimming back vines for spring.

FRANCES MAYES
UNDER THE TUSCAN SUN

Think in the morning. Act in the noon. Eat in the evening. Sleep in the night.

WILLIAM BLAKE

Roast beef Medium, is not only a food. It is a philosophy.

EDNA FERBER

We rarely repent of having eaten too little.

THOMAS JEFFERSON

My wife is a light eater. As soon as it's light, she starts to eat.

HENNY YOUNGMAN

My favorite animal is steak.

FRAN LEBOWITZ

———

It is not very easy to fix the principles upon which mankind have agreed to eat some animals, and reject others; and as the principle is not evident, it is not uniform. That which is selected as delicate in one country, is by its neighbours abhorred as loathsome.

SAMUEL JOHNSON

———

Eating while seated makes one of large size; eating while standing makes one strong.

HINDU PROVERB

I prefer the Chinese method of eating ... You can do anything at the table except arm wrestle.

JEFF SMITH

————•••••————

When it comes to Chinese food I have always operated under the policy that the less known about the preparation the better ... A wise diner who is invited to the kitchen replies by saying, as politely as possible, that he has a pressing engagement elsewhere.

CALVIN TRILLIN

————•••••————

Barbecue is more than a meal; it's a way of life.

GREG JOHNSON AND VINCE STATEN
REAL BARBECUE

Boston runs to brains as well as to beans and brown bread.

WILLIAM COWPER BRANN

Lasagna: the world's most perfect food!

GARFIELD

The nearer the bone, the sweeter the flesh.

PROVERB

Salmon are like men: too soft a life is not good for them.

JAMES DE COQUET

Give a man a fish and he has food for a day; teach him how to fish and you can get rid of him for the entire weekend.

ZENNA SCHAFFER

The rich eat the meat; the poor eat the bones.

YIDDISH PROVERB

I personally prefer a nice frozen TV dinner at home, mainly because it's so little trouble. All you have to do is have another drink while you're throwing it in the garbage.

JACK DOUGLAS

The trouble with eating Italian food is that five or six days later, you're hungry again.

GEORGE MILLER

———

Plain food is quite enough for me;
Three courses are as good as ten; —
If Nature can subsist on three,
Thank Heaven for three. Amen!
I always thought cold victual nice; —
My choice would be vanilla-ice.

OLIVER WENDELL HOLMES

I eat at this German-Chinese restaurant and the food is delicious. The only problem is that an hour later you're hungry for power.

DICK CAVETT

Dinner . . . possessed only two dramatic features— the wine was a farce and the food a tragedy.

ANTHONY POOLE

The way you cut your meat reflects the way you live.

CONFUCIUS

To retain respect for sausages and laws, one must not watch them in the making.

OTTO VON BISMARCK

What is sauce for the goose may be sauce for the gander, but it is not necessarily sauce for the chicken, the duck, the turkey or the Guinea hen.

ALICE B. TOKLAS

What hunger is in relation to food, zest is in relation to life.

BERTRAND RUSSELL

To read without reflecting is like eating without digesting.

EDMUND BURKE

To eat is human, to digest, divine.

CHARLES TOWNSEND COPELAND

One cannot think well, love well, sleep well, if one has not dined well.

VIRGINIA WOOLF

Food, Wisdom and Politics

Food is our common ground, a universal experience.

James Beard

There are few subjects that generate more home-spun wisdom, more proverbs, more opinions, and more advice than the subject of what to eat and when to eat it. How many of us have a grandmother who advises, "Eat, eat, you'll starve!" or "Finish your plate, there are starving children in the world." In addition, we are told that fish is brain food, carrots help you see in the dark, and spinach makes you strong. Of course, there is a grain of truth in all these statements; that's why even the most jaded of us find ourselves repeating these words to our own children.

Then there are those of us for whom the subject of food and diet is a never-ending battle. We have come up with hundreds of diets with one goal in mind—to stay healthy, enjoy our food and somehow find a way to stay slim, too. Diets are the subject of so much conversation and so many self-help books that they have become a formidable industry of their own.

The irony is that, for many people in the world, lack of food is still an enormous problem. Food shortages have been at the center of some of the most dramatic moments in the history of civilization. After all, what is more basic to the happiness and well-being of a country than its supply of food?

This section tries to capture the diverse ways that food is experienced throughout the world. From nutritional advice and motherly concern, to political platforms and dieting advice, follow along as our fellow travelers sum up their experiences with food.

13

Eat It, It's Good for You

Whatever will satisfy hunger is good food.

CHINESE PROVERB

———•••———

A food is not necessarily essential just because your child hates it.

KATHARINE WHITEHORN

All wholesome food is caught without a net or trap.

WILLIAM BLAKE

———

Eat little, sleep sound.

IRANIAN PROVERB

———

Be moderate in order to taste the joys of life in abundance.

EPICURUS

———

The best way to eat the elephant standing in your way is to cut it up into little pieces.

AFRICAN PROVERB

It seems odd, don't you think, that the quality of the food should vary inversely with the brightness of the lighting.

DOUGLAS ADAMS

Eat to live and not to eat.

PROVERB

The main problem in marriage is that, for a man, sex is a hunger—like eating. If a man is hungry and can't get to a fancy French restaurant, he'll go to a hot dog stand.

JOAN FONTAINE

A healthy man can go without food for two days—but not without poetry.

CHARLES BAUDELAIRE

—•◦•—

I've run more risk eating my way across the country than in all my driving.

DUNCAN HINES

—•◦•—

Food: Part of the spiritual expression of the French, and I do not believe that they have ever heard of calories.

BEVERLY BAXTER

Everything I eat has been proved by some doctor or other to be a deadly poison, and everything I don't eat has been proved to be indispensable for life. But I go marching on.

GEORGE BERNARD SHAW

I hate a man who swallows [his food], affecting not to know what he is eating. I suspect his taste in higher matters.

CHARLES LAMB

Don't dig your grave with your own knife and fork.

ENGLISH PROVERB

I certainly feel that the time is not far distant when a knowledge of the principles of diet will be an essential part of one's education.

FANNIE FARMER

Statistics show that of those who contract the habit of eating, very few survive.

WALLACE IRWIN

The food alone is adequate deterrent, unless you're very heavily into two-scoop tuna or best leather pastrami.

FREDERIC RAPHAEL
On the Warner Bros. studio commissary.

I have a great diet. You're allowed to eat anything you want, but you must eat it with naked fat people.

ED BLUESTONE

A diet is when you watch what you eat and wish you could eat what you watch.

HERMIONE GINGOLD

The best way to lose weight is to close your mouth—something very difficult for a politician. Or watch your food—just watch it, don't eat it.

EDWARD KOCH
Former mayor of New York City

Dieting: A system of starving yourself to death so you can live a little longer.

JAN MURRAY

How long does getting thin take?

WINNIE THE POOH
A. A. MILNE

You have to eat oatmeal or you'll dry up. Anybody knows that.

ELOISE KAY THOMPSON

Trying a case the second time is like eating yesterday morning's oatmeal.

LLOYD PAUL STRYKER

They are sick that surfeit with too much, as they that starve with nothing.

WILLIAM SHAKESPEARE

When a man is small, he loves and hates food with a ferocity which soon dims. But at six years old his very bowels will heave when such a dish as creamed carrots or cold tapioca appears before him.

M. F. K. FISHER

The well fed does not understand the lean.

IRISH PROVERB

I've been on a constant diet for the last two decades. I've lost a total of 789 pounds. By all accounts, I should be hanging from a charm bracelet.

ERMA BOMBECK

To always be intending to live a new life, but never find time to set about it—this is as if a man should put off eating and drinking from one day to another till he be starved and destroyed.

SIR WALTER SCOTT

The spirit cannot endure the body when overfed, but, if underfed, the body cannot endure the spirit.

ST. FRANCES DE SALES

Edible: Good to eat, and wholesome to digest, as a worm to a toad, a toad to a snake, a snake to a pig, a pig to a man, and a man to a worm.

AMBROSE BIERCE

Gentlemen do not like food that has been 'messed around with.' Continental cookery gives them diarrhea.

DOUGLAS SUTHERLAND

Food, one assumes, provides nourishment; but Americans eat it fully aware that small amounts of poison have been added to improve its appearance and delay its putrefaction.

JOHN CAGE

I want nothing to do with natural foods. At my age I need all the preservatives I can get.

GEORGE BURNS

The longer I work in nutrition, the more convinced I become that for the healthy person all foods should be delicious.

ADELLE DAVIS

The food that enters the mind must be watched as closely as the food that enters the body.

PATRICK BUCHANAN

McDonald's is a reductive kitchen for a classless culture that hasn't time to dally on its way to the next rainbow's end.

TOM ROBBINS

———

The right diet directs sexual energy into the parts that matter.

BARBARA CARTLAND

———

Tell me what you eat, I'll tell you who you are.

ANTHELME BRILLAT-SAVARIN

Dieting is murder on the road. Show me a man who travels and I'll show you one who eats.

BRUCE FROEMMING

I hate television. I hate it as much as peanuts. But I can't stop eating peanuts.

ORSON WELLES

If the English can survive their food, they can survive anything.

GEORGE BERNARD SHAW

Preserve a good constitution of body and mind. To this a spare diet contributes much. Have wholesome, but no costly food.

WILLIAM PENN

Part of the secret of success in life is to eat what you like and let the food fight it out inside.

MARK TWAIN

One should eat to live not live to eat.

CICERO

At high tide the fish eat ants; at low tide the ants eat fish.

THAI PROVERB

Often and little eating makes a man fat.

JOHN RAY

———◆◆◆———

There is no question that Rumanian-Jewish food is heavy . . . One meal is equal in heaviness, I would guess, to eight or nine years of steady mung-bean eating.

CALVIN TRILLIN

———◆◆◆———

He who cannot eat horsemeat need not do so. Let him eat pork. But he who cannot eat pork, let him eat horsemeat. It's simply a question of taste.

NIKITA KHRUSHCHEV
FORMER SOVIET PREMIER

One laughs when joyous, sulks when angry, is at peace with the world when the stomach is satisfied.

HAWAIIAN PROVERB

One man's meat is another man's poison.

ENGLISH PROVERB

I'm frightened of eggs, worse than frightened, they revolt me. That white round thing without any holes … Have you ever seen anything more revolting than an egg yolk breaking and spilling its yellow liquid? Blood is jolly, red. But egg yolk is yellow, revolting. I've never tasted it.

ALFRED HITCHCOCK

Nutrition has been kicked around like a puppy that cannot take care of itself.

ADELLE DAVIS

Nobody seems more obsessed by diet than our anti-materialistic, otherworldly, New Age spiritual types. But if the material world is merely illusion, an honest guru should be as content with Budweiser and bratwurst as with raw carrot juice, tofu and seaweed slime.

EDWARD ABBEY

More die in the United States of too much food than of too little.

JOHN KENNETH GALBRAITH
THE AFFLUENT SOCIETY

If you're going to America, bring your own food.

FRAN LEBOWITZ

The real native South Seas food is lousy. You can't eat it.

VICTOR "TRADER VIC" BERGERON

Stomachs shouldn't be waist baskets.

P. K. THOMAJAN

More people will die from hit-or-miss eating than from hit-and-run driving.

DUNCAN HINES

If your stomach disputes you, lie down and pacify it with cool thoughts.

SATCHEL PAGE

In the manner of diet, I have been persistently strict in sticking to the things which didn't agree with me until one or the other of us got the best of it.

MARK TWAIN

I see few die of hunger; of eating, a hundred thousand.

BENJAMIN FRANKLIN

It would be nice if the Food and Drug Administration stopped issuing warnings about toxic substances and just gave me the names of one or two things still safe to eat.

ROBERT FUOSS

———•❖•———

There is more simplicity in the man who eats caviar on impulse than in the man who eats Grape-Nuts on principle.

G. K. CHESTERTON

Some people have a foolish way of not minding, or pretending not to mind, what they eat. For my part, I mind my belly very studiously, and very carefully; for I look upon it, that he who does not mind his belly, will hardly mind anything else.

SAMUEL JOHNSON

The honorable and upright man keeps well away from both the slaughterhouse and the kitchen. And he allows no knives on his table.

CONFUCIUS

The second day of a diet is always easier than the first. By the second day, you're off it.

JACKIE GLEASON

The extra calories needed for one hour of mental effort would be completely met by eating of one oyster cracker or one half of a salted peanut.

FRANCIS BENEDICT

The superior man does not, even for the space a single meal, act contrary to virtue.

CONFUCIUS

Health food makes me sick.

CALVIN TRILLIN

I got food poisoning today. But I don't know when I'm going to use it.

STEVEN WRIGHT

I eat to live, to serve, and also, if it so happens, to enjoy, but I do not eat for the sake of enjoyment.

MAHATMA GANDHI

14

Season to Taste

A little bad taste is like a nice splash of paprika.

DIANA VREELAND

———◦•••◦———

A man taking basil from a woman will love her always.

SIR THOMAS MORE

Black pepper heat and comfort the brain.

JOHN GERARD'S HERBALL, 1597

A meal without salt is no meal.

HEBREW PROVERB

Tomatoes and oregano make it Italian; wine and tarragon make it French. Sour cream makes it Russian; lemon and cinnamon make it Greek. Soy sauce makes it Chinese; garlic makes it good.

ALICE MAY BROCK

As for rosemary, I let it run all over my garden walls, not only because it is the herb sacred to remembrance and to friendship, whence a sprig of it hath a dumb language.

SIR THOMAS MORE

I believe that if ever I had to practice cannibalism, I might manage if there were enough tarragon around.

JAMES BEARD

Garlic is the catsup of intellectuals.

ANONYMOUS

If I had to choose just one plant for the whole herb garden, I should be content with basil.

ELIZABETH DAVID

Sweet, sour, bitter, pungent—all must be tasted.

CHINESE PROVERB

Where would we be without salt?

JAMES BEARD

What garlic is to salad, insanity is to art.

AUGUSTUS SAINT-GAUDENS

Condiments are like old friends—highly thought of, but often taken for granted.

MARILYN KAYTOR

Pork fat rules!

EMERIL LAGASSE

You can tell how long a couple has been married by whether they are on their first, second or third bottle of Tabasco.

BRUCE BYE

There's something about garlic that creates excitement. People can get real loose around garlic.

LLOYD HARRIS
TIME MAGAZINE

There is no such thing as a little garlic.

ARTHUR BAER

Gaahlic, it's a beautiful thing!

EMERIL LAGASSE

A nickel will get you on the subway, but garlic will get you a seat.

OLD NEW YORK PROVERB

Parsley—the jewel of the herbs, both in the pot and on the plate.

ALBERT STOCKLI

It is a true saying that a man must eat a peck of salt with his friend before he knows him.

MIGUEL DE CERVANTES
DON QUIXOTE

The pungency of just-snipped herbs adds as much to the cook's enjoyment as to taste.

FRANCES MAYES

Parsley must be sown nine times, for the Devil takes all but the last.

ENGLISH PROVERB

The more you eat, the less flavor; the less you eat, the more flavor.

CHINESE PROVERB

Man can live without spices, but not without wheat.

JEWISH PROVERB

Butter is life.

INDIAN PROVERB

15

Fruit and Cheese

The weakest kind of fruit drops earliest to the ground.

WILLIAM SHAKESPEARE

————•••••————

An apple a day keeps the doctor away.

ENGLISH PROVERB

If you want to know the taste of a pear, you must change the pear by eating it yourself.

> Mao Tse Tung

———

Many's the long night I've dreamed of cheese—toasted mostly.

> Robert Louis Stevenson
> *Treasure Island*

———

You put your left index finger on your eye and your right index finger on the cheese. If they sort of feel the same, the cheese is ready.

> M. Tattinger
> On testing the ripeness of cheese

Age is something that doesn't matter, unless you are a cheese.

BILLIE BURKE

Never commit yourself to a cheese without having first examined it.

T. S. ELIOT

Poets have been mysteriously silent on the subject of cheese.

G. K. CHESTERTON

Goat cheese ... produced a bizarre eating era when sensible people insisted that this miserable cheese produced by these miserable creatures reared on miserable hardscrabble earth was actually superior to the magnificent creamy cheeses of the noblest dairy animals bred in the richest green valleys of the earth.

RUSSELL BAKER

Cheese—milk's leap toward immortality.

CLIFTON FADIMAN

How can you be expected to govern a country that has 246 kinds of cheese?

CHARLES DE GAULLE

A melon and a woman are hard to know.

SPANISH PROVERB

A watermelon will not ripen in your armpit.

ARMENIAN PROVERB

Doubtless God could have made a better berry, but doubtless God never did.

DR. WILLIAM BUTLER

We are living in a world today where lemonade is made from artificial flavors and furniture polish is made from real lemons.

ALFRED E. NEWMAN

One must ask children and birds how cherries and strawberries taste.

JOHANN WOLFGANG GOETHE

Always eat grapes downward—that is eat the best grapes first; in this way there will be none better left on the bunch, and each grape will seem good down to the last. If you eat the other way, you will not have a good grape in the lot.

SAMUEL BUTLER

Time flies like an arrow. Fruit flies like a banana.

GROUCHO MARX

All millionaires love a baked apple.

RONALD FIRBANK

Success to me is having ten honeydew melons and eating the top half of each one.

BARBRA STREISAND

Nothing raises false hope in a human being like one good cantaloupe.

ANONYMOUS

The strawberye is the wonder of all the fruites growing naturally in these partes.

SIR WALTER RALEIGH

The taste of an olive is older than meat, older than wine.

LAURENCE DURRELL

The value of those wild fruits is not in the mere possession or eating of them, but in the sight and enjoyment of them.

HENRY DAVID THOREAU

The true Southern watermelon is a boon apart, and not to be mentioned with common things. It is chief of this world's luxuries, king by the grace of God over all the fruits of the earth. When one has tasted it, he knows what the angels eat.

MARK TWAIN

Avoid fruit and nuts. You are what you eat.

JIM DAVIS, CREATOR OF GARFIELD

What are all the oranges imported into England to the hips and haws in her hedges?

HENRY DAVID THOREAU

16

What's for Dessert?

Bring on the dessert, I think I am about to die.

PIERETT BRILLAT-SAVARIN

———•••••———

Venice is like eating an entire box of chocolate liquers in one go.

TRUMAN CAPOTE

The proof of the pudding is [in] the eating. By a small sample we may judge the whole piece.

MIGUEL DE CERVANTES
DON QUIXOTE

———

They were glossed sticky dates, cold rich figs, cramped belly to belly in small boxes.

THOMAS WOLFE

———

A dessert without cheese is like a beautiful woman with only one eye.

ANTHELME BRILLAT-SAVARIN

An apple pie without some cheese is like a kiss without a squeeze.

PROVERB

Always serve too much hot fudge sauce on hot fudge sundaes. It makes people overjoyed, and puts them in your debt.

JUDITH OLNEY

Anyhow, the hole in the doughnut is at least digestible.

H. L. MENCKEN

C is for Cookie, that's good enough for me.

COOKIE MONSTER
SESAME STREET CHARACTER

———————

Cookies are made of butter and love.

NORWEGIAN PROVERB

———————

Coleridge holds that a man cannot have a pure mind who refuses apple dumplings, I am not certain but he is right.

CHARLES LAMB

———————

Life is like a box of chocolates . . . you never know what you're gonna get.

FORREST GUMP

Strength is the capacity to break a chocolate bar into four pieces with your bare hands—and then eat just one of the pieces.

JUDITH VIORST

Researchers have discovered that chocolate produces some of the same reactions in the brain as marijuana . . . The researchers also discovered other similarities between the two, but can't remember what they are.

MATT LAUER
NBC'S TODAY SHOW

You can tell a lot about a fellow's character by his way of eating jelly beans.

RONALD REAGAN

———•••———

The pie is an English institution which, planted on American soil, forthwith ran rampant and burst forth into an untold variety of genera and species.

HARRIET BEECHER STOWE

———•••———

Do you think because thou art virtuous, there shall be no more cakes and ale?

WILLIAM SHAKESPEARE
TWELFTH NIGHT

It has been shown as proof positive that carefully prepared chocolate is as healthful a food as it is pleasant; that it is nourishing and easily digested . . . that it is above all helpful to people who must do a great deal of mental work.

ANTHELME BRILLAT-SAVARIN

I couldn't remember when I had been so disappointed. Except perhaps the time I found out that M&Ms really do melt in your hand.

PETER OAKLEY

Had I but one penny in the world, thou shouldst have it for gingerbread.

WILLIAM SHAKESPEARE
LOVE'S LABOR'S LOST

What is a roofless cathedral to a well-built pie?

WILLIAM MAGINN

Older women are like aging strudels—the crust may not be so lovely, but the filling has come at last into its own.

ROBERT FARRAR CAPON

Life is uncertain. Eat dessert first.

ERNESTINE ULMER

Research tells us that fourteen out of every ten individuals like chocolate.

SANDRA BOYNTON

Very few people possess true artistic ability. It is therefore both unseemly and unproductive to irritate the situation by making an effort. If you have a burning, restless urge to write or paint, simply eat something sweet and the feeling will pass.

FRAN LEBOWITZ

She sent out for one of those plump little cakes called petite madeleines, which look as though they had been molded in the fluted scallop of a pilgrim's shell.

MARCEL PROUST
REMEMBRANCE OF THINGS PAST

Warm cookies and cold milk are good for you.

ROBERT FULGHUM

When I was a child, and the snow fell, my mother always rushed to the kitchen and made snow ice cream and divinity fudge—egg whites, sugar and pecans mostly. It was a lark then and I always associate divinity fudge with snowstorms.

It's not that chocolates are a substitute for a love. Love is a substitute for chocolate. Chocolate is, let's face it, far more reliable than a man.

MIRANDA INGRAM

Last night I dreamed of a ten pound marshmallow and when I woke up the pillow was gone.

TOMMY COOPER

17

What We Talk About When We Talk About Food

Food is our common ground, a universal experience.

JAMES BEARD

——— ❖ ———

If you are ever at a loss to support a flagging conversation, introduce the subject of eating.

LEIGH HUNT

To the ruler, the people are heaven; to the people, food is heaven.

CHINESE PROVERB

There are only two questions to ask about food. Is it good? And is it authentic? We are open [to] new ideas, but not if it means destroying our history. And food is history.

GIULIANO BUGIALLI

Grub first, then ethics.

BERTOLT BRECHT
THREEPENNY OPERA

Don't boil eggs until the hen has laid them.

ESTONIAN PROVERB

Fasting is better than prayer.

SAINT CLEMENT

The secret to staying young is to live honestly, eat slowly, and lie about your age.

LUCILLE BALL

Coarse rice for food, water to drink, and the bended arm for a pillow—happiness may be enjoyed even in these.

CONFUCIUS

It is the sign of a dull mind to dwell upon the cares of the body, to prolong exercise, eating and drinking, and other bodily functions. These things are best done by the way; all your attention must be given to the mind.

EPICTETUS

God comes to the hungry in the form of food.

MAHATMA GANDHI

There is no burnt rice to a hungry person.

PHILIPPINE PROVERB

I have clearly noticed that often I have one opinion when I lie down and another one when I stand up, especially when I have eaten little and when I am tired.

GEORG CHRISTOPH LICHTENBERG

If men do not keep on speaking terms with children, they cease to be men, and become merely machines for eating and earning money.

JOHN UPDIKE

Enough is as good as a feast.

ENGLISH PROVERB

Cutting stalks at noontime. Perspiration drips to the earth. Know you that your bowl of rice each grain from hardship comes?

CHANG CHAN-PAO

Even a melon seed may come between a husband and wife.

IRANIAN PROVERB

Do not dismiss the dish saying that it is just, simple food. The blessed thing is an entire civilization in itself.

ADBULHAK SINASI

———————

Born to the earth are three kinds of creatures. Some are winged and fly. Some are furred and run. Still others stretch their mouths and talk. All must eat and drink to survive.

LU YU

———————

Love, like a chicken salad or restaurant hash, must be taken with blind faith or it loses its flavor.

HELEN ROWLAND

America knows nothing of food, love or art.

ISADORA DUNCAN

———•·•·•———

I have a total irreverence for anything connected with society except that which makes the roads safer, the beer stronger, the food cheaper, and the old men and women warmer in the winter and happier in the summer.

BRENDAN BEHAN

———•·•·•———

I have often noticed that when chickens quit quarreling over their food they often find that there is enough for all of them. I wonder if it might not be the same with the human race.

DON MARQUIS

I think there to be no peasant in my kingdom so poor that he is unable to have a chicken in his pot every Sunday.

HENRY IV
KING OF FRANCE.

———

I've never known a country to be starved into democracy.

SENATOR GEORGE D. AIKEN

———

Philosophy! Empty thinking by ignorant conceited men who think they can digest while eating.

IRIS MURDOCH

If I were king, I would close all cafes, for those who frequent them become dangerous hotheads.

CHARLES DE MONTESQUIEU

A man who is eating or lying with his wife or preparing to go to sleep in humility, thankfulness and temperance, is, by Christian standards, in an infinitely higher state than one who is listening to Bach or reading Plato in a state of pride.

C. S. LEWIS

Eggs cannot be unscrambled.

AMERICAN PROVERB

Eggs of an hour, bread of a day, wine of a year, a friend of thirty years.

ITALIAN PROVERB

Playwrights are like men who have been dining for a month in an Indian restaurant. After eating curry night after night, they deny the existence of asparagus.

PETER USTINOV

If you think you are a mushroom, jump into the basket.

RUSSIAN PROVERB

Talk doesn't cook rice.

CHINESE PROVERB

What is patriotism but the love of the food one ate as a child?

LIN YUTANG

To eat an egg, you must break the shell.

JAMAICAN PROVERB

To eat one must chew, to speak one must think.

VIETNAMESE PROVERB

A forbidden meal is quickly eaten.

SWEDISH PROVERB

———

The holy man, though he be distressed, does not eat food mixed with wickedness. The lion, though hungry, will not eat what is unclean.

SASKYA PANDITA

———

Hunger and love are the pivots on which the world turns. Mankind is entirely determined by love and hunger.

ANATOLE FRANCE

Hunger is the best pickle.

BENJAMIN FRANKLIN

Hunger makes beans taste like almonds.

ITALIAN PROVERB

The belly rules the mind.

SPANISH PROVERB

Man does not live by words alone, despite the fact that sometimes he has to eat them.

ADLAI STEVENSON

The best food is that which fills the belly.

EGYPTIAN PROVERB

———•••••———

No man can be a patriot on an empty stomach.

WILLIAM COWPER

———•••••———

Survival is the perpetual struggle for room and food.

THOMAS MALTHUS

———•••••———

There is no bad food in time of starvation.

PHILIPPINE PROVERB

The rebellions of the belly are the worst.

FRANCIS BACON

When poets . . . write about food it is usually cele-
bratory. Food as the thing-in-itself, but also the
thoughtful preparation of meals, the serving of
meals, meals commonly shared: a sense of the sacred in the profane.

JOYCE CAROL OATES

Wish I had time for just one more bowl of chili.

KIT CARSON'S LAST WORDS

Index